Bearing Clues

Mysteries of Objects

Vivian Kearney

Bearing Clues – Mysteries of Objects
©2017, Vivian Kearney
Cover illustration © 2017, Vivian Kearney
Illustrations © 2017, Vivian Kearney and Elijah
Anzak
Pukiyari Publishers

ISBN-10: 1-63065-063-3
ISBN-13: 978-1-63065-063-6

PUKIYARI PUBLISHERS
www.pukiyari.com

Dedicated to my beloved husband Milo, our dear families, our friends, neighbors and mentors.

With many thanks to Elijah Anzak, one of our five marvelous grandsons for contributing his illustrations to this book.

With thanks to Ani Palacios, our editor, for being so helpful and patient.

And to the human creative spirit. May God, our Creator use this gift to bring joy, peace and healing on earth.

Table of Contents

Lessons

Elijah A.

What Can Objects Teach Us?

What can objects teach us?
Patience
Usefulness

Watchfulness
Metaphors, signs and symbols
Tactfully, helpfully
Offered in silence
Sparkling with possibilities

Bilingualism

A silver loose-leaf ring on a table
Right in the place where I just lost mine
But not openable, not the same
What is it trying to tell me
In its lack of usefulness?

Pieces of glitter winking on the floor
I see in many places, always
Catching the light surprisingly
What are they signaling
In their almost explicability?

Connections, perceptions, meditations
Bridges to the numinous unknown
What special language should we learn
To understand their messages
Yet not forget the daily schedule's idiom?

Camouflaged Ambassadors

Behold
Bright yellow
Sunflowers
In front of a gray fence
Trying to catch your attention
To lead you into the magic
Land of now

Objects
Camouflaged ambassadors
Await

Found Objects

Briny Brownsville

Elijah A.

Glitter Considered

The bluish points of glitter
On this page
Appear as
God's tears
When considered from a thin
Meditational place

Silver sparkles on my folder
Could have once been
Stars in a royal blue sky

Or maybe passed souls
Now flashing
Their microcosmic lights
Signaling from on high

Library Clue

Came upon
A solitary, dry
Beige and purple flower
Found pressed
Among the printed pages
Of a century-old book
Teaching how to teach
Long ago students

O, why did I close that book
So abruptly?
Before the papery bloom
Could tell its story -
Maybe whimsical
Perhaps dramatic

Where is it now?
Could I find it again?
Among myriad
Regimented shelves

It probably awaits
More appreciative eyes
To release it from the flattening past
To offer an anonymous souvenir
A sweet scent
Of a time, a mood, a relationship
Gone by...

Oh, look!
Now I've recovered it

But where will I
Put this poem?
And who
Will see it again?

Present, Yesterday

Once upon a time, yesterday
Morning a plastic bag with
A flower plant, roots and all
Was left on our lawn, near the wall

Echoing a dream of the night before
Of a rose bush; next day
On the neighboring driveway
A stern calico cat sat staring
My reactions curiously awaiting

So whose the eyes and what the plant
When spirit interpreters are not around
When strange birds fly in our skies unheeded
Their marvels by airplanes superceded

Hairpin Turn

Butterfly thoughts turned for a moment
To pick up a silver bow hairpin from the sidewalk
I captured it gently, placed it in a drawer
Where it morphed into a sparkling metaphor

Let's accept findings as smiling similes
Encouraging us to link the day's incidents
Into faith for the future, thanks for the past
Realizing that connecting presents time outlast

Don't Forget Us

The commemorative
Purple number-two pencil
Whose cheerily yellow logo:
Sunny Brownsville on the Border
Is almost whittled away

Is still sounding echoes
Of now far away
Worlds and years
Lives by the sea

December on the Table

December
On the kitchen table
Two leaves fallen
From the gifted poinsettia plant
One red, one green
Beautiful, soft and dried,

Sighing with me
Christmas is so over, alas
This year won't ever come back

Lego to Keep

Tiny, complex,
Seemingly unuseable,
Almost invisible
Blue and white Lego piece
A grandchild
With all the time in the world
Would patiently, happily
Grasp to build
A comforting war nest

That we, as grandparents
Would sighingly, helplessly
Hoard and bless

The Broken Teacup

Com-
Compart-
Compartmentalization

Why do we
Want to place
Things too neatly

In boxes, cups, bags,
Actually opposing containers,
Unwilling to admit contradictions,
Separating ideas, issues, sentiments, facts
From each other?

Once
I had a lovely teacup
With an English rose design
Its smooth alabaster shape just waiting
For some sleep-inducing
Serotonin-producing tea
Why would I want, seek or use
Any other?

Then
Something happened...
A bump by other dishes
Or a forgotten fall
Or maybe a closer inspection

And that very
Favorite container
For all my ideals and conversations,
Dreams of a comfortable social niche
Once held together by familiar buzzwords
Cracked…

Just a little…
But, alas! It wasn't perfect anymore
And couldn't be restored
To its pristine, exceptional
Glory

Digging Up the Past

Respectful archeologists
Unearth and
Brush so carefully, gently
Pottery, artifacts
That may have been
Carelessly, hurriedly, angrily
Discarded

Or, some objects may once
Have been treasured...
Prized or sanctified

Just like our recent rejects

O, who can understand
What's beneath or above
These clouds of sand?

Hoarder

On our wooden desk
Lies a white heart-shaped
Paper scrap
Torn from a notebook
Probably
Could be picked up
For fun
With a thin red string
Nearby
By some magnetic
Attraction
And be carried off
To my collection of
Found treasures

Against Stress

Like a fairy tale gift
Offered at just the right
Frenzied moment
At the workplace

The lotion tube so long lost
Reappeared in my purse and advised
Apply me
To pressure points
On your arm and forehead
Against the problems of the day

And I will emanate
Good will and serotonin
And peppermint peacefulness

A little present - *un regalito*
From *Diosito*
Siempre presente -
God always here

Transported

While rearranging my yellow room
A hypnotic turquoise-colored pencil
Called me, calls me

Urging me to be ready
To draw and fly with
Blue-green birds, grasses and flowers
And jump into the whimsical dimension
Of a turquoise earth and sky

A Wink and a Nod

An important button found
Thread to match
Needle just right, although
All were recently
Hopelessly scattered

Serendipity so helpful
A heavenly wink and nod
For life-changing events
And small enough matters

A Green Cardboard Key

Walking, pondering
In an oak-lined parking lot
Towards a wardrobe-regenerating store

I spied a green cardboard key
Maybe sent to open
A paper door

Of mysterious family histories
That has been shut
That I close
So relentlessly…
Depressingly

Maybe it's a text message
Linking the encouraging sky
To gray concrete

Announcing, advising
That creativity, charity,
And sweet serendipity
Are some comforting,
Living answers

Life of Artifacts

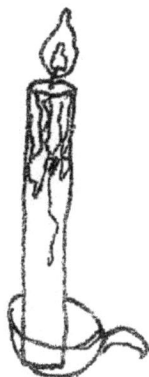

Elijah A.

Third Grade Sticker Heaven

Tiny, cute, pink and blue birds singing *Well Done!*
Miniature Santa Clauses announcing *To* and *From*
Iconic rainbows giving goals for tomorrow
Sticker albums of childhood's glow

Wielke Oczy

The tag taken off
The to-be-recycled ringbinder
Wielke Oczy —
Little Polish long ago *shtetl*
Dear old village of family legends

Sticks to my hand
And won't
Let
Go

Paper Tab Emperor

Carlos Quinto
Do you shudder
And shiver when

You realize
We now write, paste, and reorganize
Into our useful ringbinders
For our teaching agendas

Minute paper tabs
With your name
Calmly categorizing
Your rule, policies, armies
Once panoplied and feared
All over Europe?

Kitchen Decorations

Rice-paper thin, rose-like
The present of a golden moth orchid's
Faded, jaded blooms reminisce gently
Quietly on the corner table

A gift of the Nativity in a rough coconut shell
Texas wild flowers on blue plastic plates all around
the room
A toy copper kettle wondering about its mission
A basket of plastic fruits assuring near nutrition

Skylight, cloudlight portraying the weather
Knicknacking souvenirs for children to handle
A tan cowboy hat resting near a terra-cotta bas-relief
of Mary
A brass *menorah* candleholder to recall miracles and
mercies

Attitudes

Certain household
Articles, items
Definitely electronics

Sometimes act like
Recalcitrant students
Not working well
Loving to trip
And waste hours
Eager to distract

While others
Follow instructions easily
Doing needed tasks
With a positive attitude

At the right place
In good time

Their Own Home

Put
Things away
In a contented place

Don't let them
Groan, moan and nag
Too much

For their own
Restful, helpful,
Happy home

Mythical Housekeeping

Housekeeping as Sisyphean
Housecleaning as Zeno's arrow
Maybe Greek housewives of antiquity
Made up those evocative myths

The boulders of chores keep rolling down
Dusty clutter gathers high and low
Penelope-like, undoing what's done before
And never do I reach my low-bar goal

Transition and Adoption

A scrap of paper
Had been
Lying so long on our lawn
Trying to camouflage itself
In the grasses and weeds

That it became
A leaf-like parchment
Perfectly adapted
To the welcoming ground
Announcing fuzzily
Pepsi refreshment was here

Abandoned houses and objects
Witness the people who made them,
Used them, left them
To their own conversations
With sun, moon and sky
And the earth that
Finally adopts them

Distractions

Pressing, entreating
Planned so wisely
Chores and wonderful projects
Clamoring-to-be-organized objects
You are persuading me, distracting me
To disregard that it's the end of
This summer

Now
What happens to
Procrastination's
Lilting, confusing melodies
Deceptively promising
Lovely and endless
Time?

On the Surface

Surfaces
Floors, blinds, shelves
Counters, couches, beds
Lamps, books, souvenirs
Countless more
To dust
Star powder, skin cells
Away from our
Fragile lungs

Visions of Mortality

Candle,
Whispering nightwinds,
Tell me a story
A vision
Of this earthly life
As it burns
Down

Companions

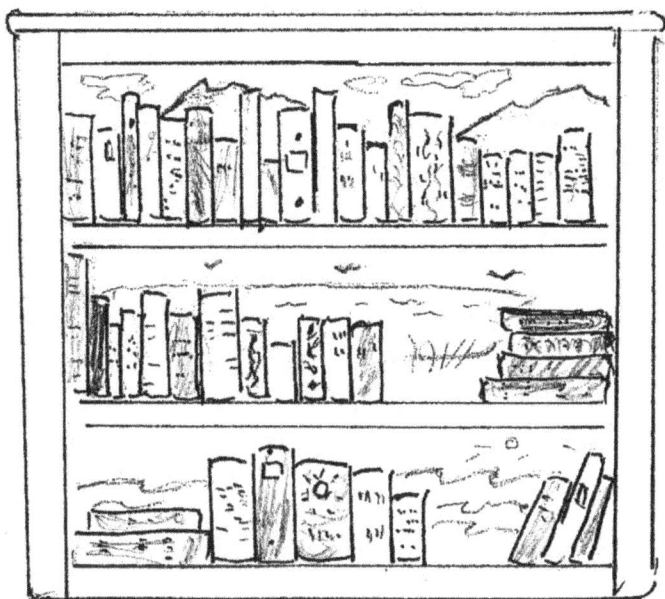

Biographical Clothes

Ironing the evening
Unfolding the feelings
An uncreased white blouse glows
Like a starry night's snow

Wonderful how
Yesterday's clothes
Review our biographies

Vivian Kearney

Street Person Found in the Library

Books were his family
His friends, his neighbors
The library was his home
His planetarium, his shelter

What were his reflections
His meditations, his ruminations
As his soul prepared to float
Above the library, to the knowing heavens

Connections – Matthew 9:20, 21

`

Fringes, fringe benefits
Fringes everywhere
On mats, scarves, blankets, clothes
On prayer shawls

A fringe linking its woven cloth
To a desperate soul
Trying to touch
The hem of Jesus

Vivian Kearney

Number Them

Heart patterns
On flannel pyjamas
Count them
To battle the windmills
Of insomnia
To get back
To healing sleep

Then number
The amazing
Merciful graces
You were granted
Instead of
Nondescript sheep

Reflected

The ghost of a computer icon
The shadow of its wings
Blue, yellow, red and green
Reflected on a puzzled glass
Near window pane

Tries to impersonate
A four-color butterfly
That quickly flies away
With the calming, psalming
Mauve twilight

Relating or Not

Moving in natural time
People can relate to
Cathedrals, cultural heritage
And aren't lonely

Guarded by clocks
People tear down cathedrals
And can't talk
For the invisible walls
That surround them

Playing with virtual space
People are pulled into
The flat, manipulable screen
Promising eternal friendship
Of ether's uncaring
Ghosts

The Newspaper's Ad Asks

Wouldn't you like to see
On your smart ultra HDTV
Almost three-dimensional
In your world
All the bright colors
The complex patterns
Of this *Art Nouveau*
Chandelier?

Wait a minute
My grumpy eyes ask
We think that
This incredibly beautiful
Glass skylight
Is on the ceiling
Of a Paris department store
Not in our malls

No, responds the Internet
It's part of
The Barcelona
Music Palace
Concert hall

Anyways…
Why can't we decide
To make and have
In tangible reality

Vivian Kearney

Such awesomely
Intricate artifacts
In our neck of the woods
Here?

Internet Conspiracies

They
Want us to develop
ADD propensities

Having us
Read the news, interrupted
By multiple red herrings
And rabbit trails unending
Pointing in all directions
For distracted
Unfocused surfing

Not especially
Interested in
Presenting important knowledge
For true change

Towards progressive fairness

Trail

A book is a walk
A walk with the author
Sooner or later
Your thoughts fall in step

A book is a ray
From another planet
Sometimes giving comfort
With its different light

A book is a dream
Into unknown yet mapped
Territories giving you practice
For your waking ventures

God's two books
The bible and nature
Can be

Keys to His kingdom
Rivers of many rests

Books Beckoning

Our bookcases have been moved
With their denizens. The garage
Rejoices to become
A library, temporarily
Housing nests of knowledge

While the bared white living room walls
With their blue-framed windows
Wait impatiently to be restored
To our books' far horizons

Reconciliation

This popcorn paint facing me, surrounding me
Maybe the hurried painters used for frugality
First seemed so ugly to touch, to see
But now looks like stars, scattered unpredictably

Wonderful how metaphors can reconcile
And work against vexations for a while
Opening boxes of paradigms unlikely
Calming some objects' trials pleasantly

Let's Applaud God

A creaky horizontal curtain
The metal garage door
Opens

To an airy street vista
Of sunbeams greeting
Trees, yards and houses

Ready to start
The play of a day
Let's applaud God

Microcosmic Visitor

Visiting
Speck of dust
Tiny and white
Floats around
Like a lost miniature spaceship
Wandering through the room's
Universe

Planetary Icon

Dusty old globe
Twirlable
Moveable
Faded icon

In our living room
On our planet
Orbiting in its own
Galactic dance halls

Vivian Kearney

Quis Custodiet Custodies?

If a tree falls in the forest
Is there a sound
If no one cares?

If a car beeps in the parking lot
Signaling some alarm
Yet no one turns around
Or pays any mind
Does its noise disappear
Without a trace?

If someone disparages you
What happens to self?
Is it still esteemed?
And who will redeem?

If a grudge is not nourished
If a criticism flies unheeded
Can it be dismissed
And not much missed?

Quis custodiet custodies?
Who will guard the guardians?
Who will sing God's mercy?
Who will enable us to live
By God's Holy Spirit of love
For His glory?

Certain Curtain Folds

Certain moods
Float like clouds
Grazing like sheep
In cumulus pastures
Of pale blue skies

Certain sadnesses,
Worries, debilitating pains
Weigh like crosses
Difficult to bear
And keep on walking

Certain tunnelled curtain folds
Like some good words
Let the light shine through
At the end of their paths
Portraying hopes
For brighter tomorrows

Art Mirrors

Maxwell Parish Painting

The playful moon,
Possibly smiling, peeks
From behind a tree

To shed its golden beams
On party preparations

By identically clothed clowns
Arranging moon-shaped lanterns
Glowing in competition

SAMA Museum – Statue of A Woman Pleading

Her hands reach out to Christ's feet
But look – her fingers are broken
A space forever between
Unable to touch —
Crying

At The Southwest School of Art

Neon-apple-green the lovely room
Black, white, wood, gray, aqua
The rest of the of the color scheme
Empty except for branched lamps
And us

Elsewhere the chapel
Void of chairs but glistening
The polished floor, the slightly smudged
Stained windows, some from Ireland
A tiny wardrobe room in the back
With two mirrors placed at angles
So we could see our full reflections
Five times

Footsteps of far-away voices
Of students and administrators
Preparing an art show
A summary of art classes week
For us

Story at a Retreat

The painting on the pine wood wall
Of the story-telling, inspirational retreat
Pictures a *rebozo*-shawled lady
Holding a bouquet of flowers
Waiting in a bus depot
With those conventional red plastic chairs

White plaster the picture's wall
And floors and echoing white
Her suitcase of hope

Quiet the patience of the traveler
Contrasted with the violent movement
Of the poster behind her

So often used by Spanish teachers
To decorate their classrooms
Of a bullfight
On the wall
Prayerfully behind her

Of Some Fame

Emphasizing
Perspective, texture
Or light, lines, design, color
Shapes and/or shadows

Impressionistically
Or abstractedly
Or emotionally
Or fantastically
Or photographically
Realistically

A painting
Carefully
Or impulsively
Finished
Or left undone

Calls up a picture
Of a creative
Marveling being

Who left us
To our too human
Categorizing
Criticizing

Who will appreciate the effort?
And who painted the painter?

Vincent Van Gogh's Gift

Starlit night
Shimmering fields
Pulsing sun
Nature's colors, movements
Beating down

The lonely soul
Pushed to translate that beauty
To sublimate the passion
Into the two dimensional
World of canvas

Paintings
That became
Our relatives,
Our Western art mantras

Look at them and see
The gifts of light
Appreciate the translator

And worship
The Giver

Medieval Artistry

Breathtaking
Those puzzle-patterned
Cathedral windows
Celebrating the butcher, baker, tanner
Knight, merchant, ruling family
The many working
Worshipping together
On the great edifice
With jeweled glass dedicated
To God, the artistic Creator

Expense sought rather than spared
Loving details worked into
All materials
The slowly developed building
A medieval devotional
Rather than our quick, boxed
Modern pragmatic

Clothes, Hobbies, Toys and Gadgets

Elijah A.

Early Baptism Gown

Photographs
From
Early in the life
Of baptismal-costumed babies

Let others know
How cherished, protected
Those children's start

And mostly
The moment stays, radiates
Opens later chances

May all children
(Youths and adults)
Be blessed
With a fair share
Of good clothes
Of support
Of loving care

Mothering Practice

Do seven-year old girls cherish
Love and care for their dolls?

Yes, o yes
Modeled one young church visitor
Patiently rearranging
Her charge in the pew
Not getting angry
When it kept falling over

The doll was warmly
And conservatively dressed
The girl wore a glittery top,
And sparkly *Ugg* boots

Young fashionista concerns
Co-existing with maternal roots

Interest Group

I wonder
Who bought the same jacket
I did
Answering the same need
Lending the same mood
Made in the same factory

Maybe we should meet
Maybe we should have
An app
For that

Lost

Heartbroken, the thrown around
Disrespected clothes leave
To their own hidden Nirvana
Sometimes persuaded back
By contrite prayers

Scattered poem lines fly away
Tired of being parked for later use
They disappear among synapses and stars
Sometimes returning as fireflies

Lost on our shores we try
To build sandcastle memorials
To those who once shared our roads
And now sail on shrouded waves
To heavens of no return

The Glass Shoes Versus Plato's Shoes

In the particular it's true
Cinderella was the one and only
To dance in those mythical glass shoes
What none other could do

But the general idea and reality
Of protective footwear
Is platonically out there

An abstract recipe
For every person's
Walking, dancing needs

Once It Was Lydia Pinkham's Vegetable Tonic

Mother's little helpers
Supervisors' rest
Keeps kids, adults
Cozily occupied
In whatever nest

With I-electronic
Interaction constant
So fascinatingly,
Fashionably changeable

A modern trade-off for
Disappearing skills sociable

Novel Entertainment

First it's a bicycle
That I can ride leisurely
Then stop and walk
In the non-fiction world

Then it's a car
That zooms me faster
Through the make-believe
Scenery

Then I'm on a ship
Complete with its own
Social world that
I seem to be able
To join

Then it's a roller-coaster ride
Addicting me to the adrenalin
Of reading faster
To the closure

Is that a good thing?
Will that novel extend, inform
My real present of a life?

Waiting to be Archived

The photos not scrapbooked
And beribboned
Seem bedraggled now
Waiting for redemption somehow

Outdated

Monopoly of acquisition
Scrabble of naming
Chess of competition
Bingo of recognition

Puzzle of arrangement
Plastic soldiers strategizing
Fuzzy books foldouts
Cards of doubt

With the computer's
Cool brain games
They're all out

For children of technology
Nothing in the house
Is as captivating, fascinating
As the tap, tap, tapping
Of an ever-ready mouse

At the Gym

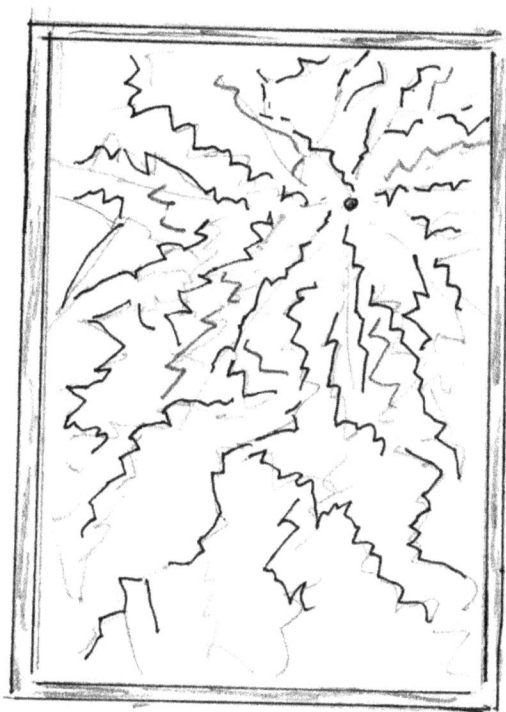

Breakage

Who knew
That glass once fragmented
Could sparkle in such
Filigreed branches
Encrypting a bemusing pattern,
A webbed galaxy
Underneath its deceptively
Smooth surface of

A shattered window,
With nervous lines radiating
Still holding
The pane

Electric Owls

Lamps reflected in the high windows
Of our very energetic gym
Receding above the hilly cityscape
Wink like angelic electric owls
From the clouds

Do they look at us looking at them?
Are they ghosts dreaming with us
For more perfect futures
In a wiser, kinder
More peaceable world?

Miraging Jar

In a certain light
On the gym patio
A glossy brown jar
Holding a fan-shaped
Butterfly palm
Starts arranging
Its shadows
Channeling

A narrow converging street
In a virtual village
With miniature housewives scurrying
On multi-shop errands
Under flowered window ledges...

Then
As the sun moves on
The mirage slips quickly back
To its glazed
Plant-container identity

And the village people
Fly back to an invisible dimension
Perhaps still real

Northern Lights in the Southwest

Reflections on the moving waters
Of the swimming pool create
Shadowy wave patterns
Shimmering, dancing on the yellow wall

Looks like northern lights
Coming to pay southern neighbors
A friendly call
A generous invitation
To global celebration

Architecture Mentors

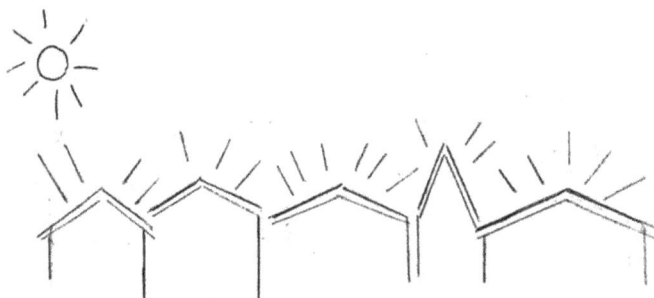

Refuge

Architecture!
A hearth for dreams,
A temple for daily living, working, learning,
A safe place,
For relationships, projects, entertainment and habits,
A haven for possessions,
Property's flag,
Refuge ministry

Architecture!
Soaring as trees,
Cozy as caves,
Reassuringly compartmentalizing
With its rooms,
Walled like a shell

Architecture!
Nests with feathers of thought,
Engineered copies of nature,
And our protection from the same

Architecture...
Practicing here for
A future peaceable
Kingdom of souls

A vision of
A holy city of gold

Parked at our Grandsons' School

Oak branches form gray
Shadows on a beige stucco wall
Silvery leaf shapes
Morph into ghosts of birds
Not quite singing
In this second dimension

All is quiet, moved
Only by the spirit
Of a gentle, invisible wind

Shadows and minutes cry
O when will
Multidimensional, symphonical
Miracles be sent
To our planet
Again?

Easter Bonnets

Newly minted, redone
Bonneted roofs
Red and blue, gray, green
Brown and tan
Gleam proudly in the sun

Months after a city-wide hailstorm
Peeled patches of the old

Now we're weather-wise
They silently proclaim
Ready for
Twenty more Easters

For a Warm Home

The house needs mothering
At least nursing twelve/seven
Or it turns surly, conspiring
With dirt and clutter
To reveal its inner
Neglected child

Let us now
With the twin needles
Of time and space
Knit for it

A warm coat,
Of many colors,
Dressing it favorably
Cleaning it regularly

But quickly, before
Lack of energy,
Other interests,
Or plain puttering
Unravel the pattern's
Ideal

More Housecleaning Hints

Pretend each cornered
Square foot is a world
With its own straggly archeology
Waiting to be dusted, rearranged
Into one overarching artifact
For the present

No, Me First

At the crossroads
Of the hall
What room
To survey
To attend to

Which is calling
The most desperately
Saying God says
Work with me first

Tell you what
To make it fair
Why not before
Doing anything

Write a poem
About cleaning, organizing
To begin

To start

Vivian Kearney

Somebody's Kitchen

Go into someone's kitchen
And you'll feel like
An unknowing *novia,*
A new bride wandering
Around in an unfamiliar place

This done, cooked another way
That stored, mapped differently

Good thing women's magazines
Generously offer their *abuelita* advice,
Grandmotherly tips,
To rightly keep and carry on
This society's practical, sweet traditions

Feng Shui Ideals

Houseful of rooms and corners
Where objects play
Orienting *Feng Shui*
And positional checkers
With waiting spaces

Both working to arrange
Comforting places
Making them useful
Intertwining, moveable
Enjoyable house-scapes

Gray Slum Flat

On the rickety marvelous steps
Of our gray slum flat
Gracing a tumbled down porch
On Montreal's City Hall Street

Bundle after language-teaching bundle,
A treasure trove of comic books —
Our gateway to the new North American life

We once perused until twilight
Called us back to our immigrant culture

Mansion on Craig Street

A patient, sunlit quiet place
A disintegrating abandoned mansion
Neglected for years

Welcomes pigeons perching happily
Among its tired columns
Windows crookedly venetian-blinded
Brown grass expecting an unknown gardener
Bushes and trees of the so-tended
Next yard waving commiserating leaves

Upscale locations around try to ignore
This uncouth, undwelt neighbor
That just awaits a renewing kiss
Of a caring, moneyed prince

Contents of Houses

There are always doubts dancing in the kitchen
There are always fears floating in the halls
There are always pains pouncing in doorways
May you have courage over them all

There are always sorrows slinking on porches
There are always regrets raining in the garden
There are always mistakes messing up tables
May you have courage over them all

There are always knots nagging in studies
There are always questions sighing on couches
There are always wearinesses weeping on rooftops
God give you courage over all

Sanctuary

The church building is made of
Bricks of tears, rafters of sighs,
Insightful lights,
Windows of prayers, cushions of ties

Highways and Byways, City and Streets

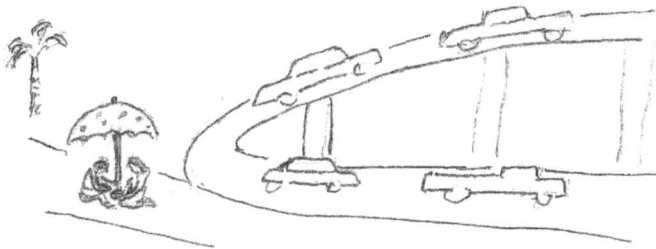

Elijah A.

We Meet Again

Where do your ghosts still walk the streets?
Where do your molecules remember to hover?
Where do your ancient feelings meet you at corners?
Where do previous conversations still hum?

Houses and streets, city and country skies
Former clothes and drawings, events and songs
Old photos, books, rooms, objects still talking
That can't quite say their final goodbyes

San Antonio's Loops 410 and 1604

Two lassos around this town
And many spokes radiating outwards
Towards cowboy country, wagon wheel history
Alamo echoes, trailing iconic memories

Vivian Kearney

Toggle the Streets

Toggle the streets from Thursday to Sunday
They flower with neon signs announcing
Marvelous yard, garage, rummage, estate sales
Of treasures for kind adoptions waiting

Toggle the house and it transforms
From taciturn walls to talkative company
Exchanging silences for symphonies of conversations
Jokes, songs, comments, and shared philosophies

Highways and Byways of San Antonio

Know me
Memorize my stops and ramps
Recognize my buildings and landmarks
Understand my twists and turns
Enjoy the hills and dales

And then I might
Show you signs
To tell you my names —
Or… maybe not —
That's my game

Known Routes

I know this route
The car does also

Its atoms mixing
With the familiar air
Above the oft-pictured
Landmarks and pavements

My molecules reside
With its trees, bushes and buildings
And they hold me, surround me
Safely

Unlike the unknown ways
Where directions are muddled
Traffic threatens and

Doesn't allow me to stop
Or slow down
To reorient

And all visible and invisible says
We're not acquainted
And you're getting
Lost

That Was Some Time Ago

When
The streets were infinitely ongoing
And portrait-present

When
Each landmark
Slowly became
A familiar corner
And each corner
A harbinger of possibilities

When
We didn't know
The ramifications
Of locations

We wandered, lost
Rejoicing
In the new city

Racing Through Time

At night the cars on Highway Ten
Red/white lights send
Like a parade
Always replayed

At night the travellers await
Their destined date
For time is space
In this world's race

Christmas Walks in Montreal

City in the seas
Of my memory

You have become
Snapshots of
Houses of snow
On winding and hilly
Cote St Catherine road

Each house fronted
By a live lit pine tree
Sparkling in a single
Twinkling color
Red or blue, gold,
Green or white

That I would walk by dreamily
Enjoying the free stories
Those Christmas trees told

Illuminating my ongoing strolls
Around the pilgrim-friendly city

Christmas Drive in San Antonio

The splishes of rain
The splashes of colors
Purple, red, green, gold
Pools on the thirsty pavements

A gallery of impressionistic paintings
For the price of a drive

Country Western Style

Galloping down the Texas highway
Cloud islands smiling in pale blue skies
Country singer slow crooning
Eternal hellos and constant goodbyes

Gazing at the city's skyscapes
Proud of landmark recognition
Watching other cars parallel ride
Then veer into corners unknown

May our southwest song be far from over
Though it started some decades ago
Soon modern cars will gallop without drivers
With new tech tunes sweet and low

Vivian Kearney

The Beautiful Being

The city, the beautiful being
Snores in its sleep
With far away sporadic roars
Trucks, cars, motorcycles its cells
Travelling through its arteries

The artificial lights
For its nocturnal eyes
Or shimmering dreams

Awaiting the awakening sun

On the Side of the Highway

Purple
Polka dot
Embracing umbrella

Shelters
The visiting couple
Crouched side by side
On the side
Of the highway

Counting money
Recounting
Under the summer-hot
Setting sun

What do you think
Of this big city
That you walked to,
Walked so long through?

Can gold be found
On or under
The streets stretching
Their enticing palms?

Sidewalks and Beyond

Grey
Sidewalks keep
Us in step with...
Connected to
Adult thinking

But all that asphalt
Doesn't help us
Sense the ghost birds
The spirit clouds
Floating above

And beyond the streets'
Perceptions and grids

That playful children
Measure knowingly
With white chalk

Marking where
The regimentation
Ends
And intuition
Begins

The Dawning Christmas Street

So hushed
So still
So colorfully lit
This dawning Christmas street
Gives beautiful thanks
A December morning place
Of worship

Meeting

While you're wandering
                Around
The lonely streets
                Of your heart

Jesus, your Creator, Comforter
                Savior
Walks over to meet
                And greet you
And welcome you
                To His house

Be of good courage

Don't be afraid to journey
                With Him

And accept
                His gracious invitation

Just Visiting

Elijah A.

The Alamo

Young
Dagger palm
Its sharp leaves
Wrapped around the
Hundred and fifty year old
Oak tree

Whose leaves
Weave
A canopy
For the ghosts
Of the fallen heroes
Of the Alamo

Taj Mahal

Marble tears for a lost bride
Monument of grief for all to see
A friendship so wondrous to behold
Building a memorial most lovely

More perfect than the Taj Mahal,
God's new Jerusalem
Is not wrought in sorrow, but built with gladness
The whole city will be as shining white glass
And round about, behold, the river of many rests

Tour Bus

Through a bus' window
Touring a familiar-foreign land
How beautiful the sights
Can be
That we don't see
Past our own
Self-reflections

Visiting England

The singing stones
The echoing lights
The battle-worn flags
The praying inscriptions
The dancing tracery
The veined ceilings
The meditating cloister

Remembering a hero
Fighting a death

Waiting at San Antonio's Incarnate Word University

Taste
The ringing bells
Listen
To the wafting clouds
Touch
The beloved breath beside me
See
What hasn't been
Perceived before

Four angels with golden trumpets
On the detailed tower
A cloud in the form of a high-heeled shoe
Strolling in the high blue skies
White, bone-smooth as clay
Sculpted trunks and branches
A lamp-post with a hidden compartment
At its iron base
Playful dune buggies transporting
Serious future students around this downtown campus

Red brick the quiet
Leafy green the metaphors
Encouraging the learning
Light receiving
We should all honor and
Strive for

Touring Around Civilizations

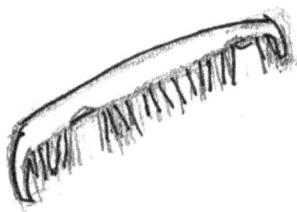

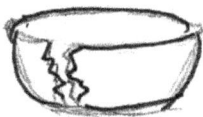

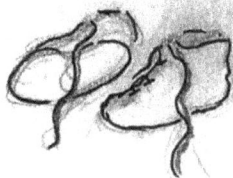

Object Museum

Touring around civilizations
That roared and were stilled
That fashioned and traded
Objects small and grand
A many-cathedralled trip
Through otherwise
Abstract history

Observing our multitudinous
Human talents

Witnessing that
Some/many were hoping
That our skillful, artistic
Though dysfunctional
Family of man
Could be calmed enough
To create, to appreciate

To hold hands together
To be healed forever

Don Quijote, Bouvard and *Pecuchet*, Museums

What you made fun of, Flaubert
With your Quijotesque adventures
Of Bouvard and Pecuchet characters
On their impossible quest
For encyclopedic familiarity
With a world of objects

Encompassing museums
Curate, explicate, celebrate —

The windmills have been tamed

Objects as Mourners

The soft blue lace-up shoe of a child
Scuffed and pummelled, left behind
Before the gas took its owner
Lets generations later understand much more
What happened to fellow humans before

Speak, sad shoes, tell us
How with high hopes you were fashioned
How your happy usefulness was cut off
So wildly, and you acquired
A longer-lived mourners' mission

Internet News from Auschwitz

Artifacts continue to surface
Each surviving object —
A toy, a bowl
A comb, a button,
A death camp uniform
A testimony, evidence
Of its owners'
Assassination by racial
Prejudice

May these tragic finds
Keep admonishing us
To honor our once
Family, neighbors

To keep present
Souls, bodies and belongings together

To remember to pray that
We all live thankfully,
Caringly, joyfully
Here and forever

Can We Hear

Objects whisper
Truths about our culture
In a world full
Of other noises

…Come closer

Hyphens

Spiritual sky
Material world
Joining them both
Questing words

Telling us to look
At objects as hyphens
Between what is sensed
And signs of salvation

Visions of Immortality

Morning to morning
Air settles
On objects whispering
On creation talking

Trying to catch your attention
After a loss
With bird cries and murmuring waters
Strangely accompanying butterflies
Stars made of tears
Clouds of sighs
Tunes from beyond

God is sending you
Your beloved's gaze
Your passed relative's thoughts
Your friend's dreams

Suddenly you find
Lamps for your quests
Paths for your day
Strength to breathe

Listen to God's angels
Synchronicity and serendipity

Moving space, time,
Words, actions, events
And objects

To become signs
That relay the immortal love
Of never disappearing souls

Vivian Kearney

Wings

Objects, artifacts, architecture, things
Each with a value, a mission to sing
Mysteries around everywhere
If we could just see their wings

Bringing Gifts

For the winter baby
They brought
Precious objects —
Gold, frankincense, myrrh
Clues from afar

That Mary pondered: why these
Why for a king, why for God
Why to overcome
The smell of death
And whence the pointing star